ADVANCE PRAISE FOR

OUT TAKES/ GLOVE BOX

"Maya Jewell Zeller's poems bite back. In lush, lyrical lines, she describes the sensuality of the natural world and the blistering challenge-dream of motherhood and cishet marriage. The contrast between freedom found in nature, in friendship, in solitude; and the weight of social expectations unravels at the touch of a body (of work) so expansive it lends its blood to make new hearts. Throughout this collection, poems morph from roots to trunks to dandelions blown, softness scattered across the field: 'I want / to share this square of blue. Let's fuck / up the room.' These are courageous, captivating poems by a poet unafraid to tell the truth about her life."

— **CAROL GUESS**, author of *Book of Non* and *Sleep Tight Satellite*

"Zeller's *out takes/glove box* is a desk with so many cubbyholes, a hawthorne tree on which each bud is dark pink and then lighter pink and then white and you can't believe the intricacy and secrets you might have missed. These poems list images that are beautiful and interesting as they fly by, but then are zoomed in on individually to reveal more: the speaker's 'used little ovaries,' the horse she cut open, her 'glove box full of dirt.' My favorite part of this book is the poetry of its structure: like a life, it opens and closes with out-takes, images that collect inside all of us before we have language, images that get neglected or forgotten for a while in the middle, while our speaker is busy being a mother and a myth, so those images must be returned to again: that rhododendron, that 'small, smoldering dress.'"

— **LAURA READ**, author of *But She Is Also Jane*

newamericanpress
*
Milwaukee, Wisconsin

out takes/ glove box

Printed in the United States of America
ISBN 978-1-941561-31-7

Cover and Book Design + Collages by Angelo Maneage

For ordering information, please contact:
Ingram Book Group
One Ingram Blvd.
La Vergne, TN 37086
(800) 937-8000
orders@ingrambook.com

For media and event inquiries, please visit:
WWW.NEWAMERICANPRESS.COM

OUT TAKES/ GLOVE BOX

MAYA JEWELL ZELLER

newamericanpress

CONTENTS

13 FIELD GIRL COME HOME

*

17 DOCUMENTARY

19 OUT-TAKES FROM THE MAKING:

I. MY USED LITTLE OVARIES

II. THE HORSE WE OPENED TOGETHER

III. THIS DARK BOX/WHAT ABOUT THE MOTHS?

IV. THE ROADS I DROVE

V. A CITY OF PETALS

VI. THIS OLD CAR

VII. ITS RUSTED AXLE

VIII. BACK ROADS, WINDING, NO GRID

*

31 THE ORIOLE OUTSIDE MY WINDOW REMINDS ME

33 A LOVE STORY

35 STILL LIFE WITH MATERNAL INSTINCTS

36 ODE TO ALL THE WOMEN WHO WALK INTO THE LAKE AND SOME OF THE WOMEN WHO TAKE THEIR CHILDREN WITH THEM

38 "WHATEVER GETS THE HAY DOWN TO THE PONIES"

39 STORY PROBLEMS

40 JAKE, THE ALLIGATOR MAN

*

45 IN THOSE EARLY DAYS, THE WOMAN WHO WAS A MERMAID DREAMS OF LONELINESS

46 WHEN SHE SWAM AMONG HORSES

48 WHEN THEY SCANNED HER BRAIN FOR LOVE

49 GARDEN THERAPY: SHE GROWS ASPARAGUS
50 IN ART THERAPY, THEY HAVE HER SKETCH LEGS
52 JANUARY 9, 1493: COLUMBUS MISTAKES MANATEES FOR MERMAIDS

*

57 BOWL OF CLOCKS AND STONES
59 SPELL FOR RE-MAKING THE PERSONAL ENVIRONMENTAL IMAGINATION
61 SPELL FOR EXTROVERSION
63 SPELL FOR THE FACE OF TERRY SAWCHUK (1966) & FOR MEDUSA NEBULA
67 ELLENSBURG IS THE WINDIEST MONTH: APRIL EDITION (SPELL FOR AURALOGY)
68 SPELL FOR THEIR BELLY BUTTONS/ WITH A DICTIONARY CLOGGING ITS WINDPIPE
71 SPELL FOR HIGHLY CAPABLE CHILDREN/ & NEWBORN GIRAFFES / & GAFFES

*

75 OUT-TAKE AS A DREAM OF CHILDREN
77 OUT-TAKE AS A CURL OF DUSK
78 OUT-TAKE AS A SONNET OF WAR
79 OUT-TAKE AS A DREAM OF RHODODENDRON
81 OUT-TAKE AS A NARROW DRESS
83 OUT-TAKE/ STORYBOARD

85 ACKNOWLEDGMENTS
87 NOTES

OUT TAKES/ GLOVE BOX

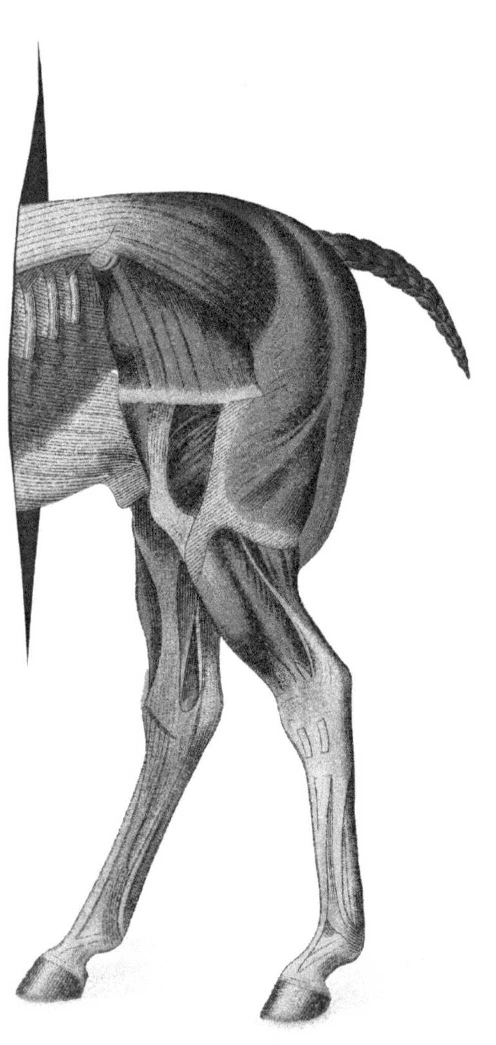

FIELD GIRL COME HOME

You float out cow-tipping   in your white gown,
          the river seldom following its old course.

They say the barn is haunted   with the ghosts
          of horses. Your metal ring, a dog howling

at clouds. Those games you feign   in daylight
          hide in the wood pile, clothes torn,

palms damp, throats closed.   You know
          the rules. You broke them. You gleam past

the bovines in their tight hides.   They say
          a river erodes six inches of its banks

each year. Here's the old mud hole.   *This*
          is the moment   *you learn what you'll love.*

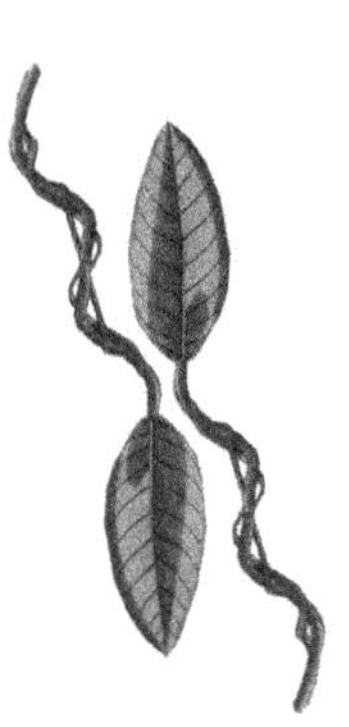

*

Mother, I am
out of my mind, spilling everywhere.

ROBIN EKISS

DOCUMENTARY

On the screen, my brain's
    bright jewelry, arranged
in a love scene:

my mother, my used
    little ovaries, this dark box,
the roads I drove.

I am making a city
    of petals, of rhododendrons,
places I can arrive.

I drove here on the roads
    of my brain, the gray streets,
the creases of my mother.

I drove here in this old car,
    with its rusted axle
and its peeling steering wheel

and its glove box full of dirt.
    Around me, chestnuts fall
from their mothers,

from their dark
    driving forces. In the field
where I have arrived,

I close the horse
    we opened together.
I close its flayed stomach,

hinged and winged
    like moths, its wet little eggs
still bobbing in their soft ponds.

My equine anatomy.
    My horse-mother. My four footed
beast. I ride her back home.

OUT-TAKES FROM THE MAKING:
I. MY USED LITTLE OVARIES

still full,
still braided rivers, those vessels

of salt, blood, follicles

afraid of the light —

this oocyte opera

wants to be a baby

wants to be a city

of limbs

you say silly city

silly permeable myometrium

silly reproductive system

of infinite destruction
in which every month someone dies

in this vermilion funeral

II. THE HORSE WE OPENED TOGETHER

with our knives
with our blood swell
            like plump cells
            like a boy part: surge

with our eggy mixers

with our barbed little vaginas

oh dangerous as hell

we cut her, throat
to belly to rear

and her entrails whole and
            whorl, her little moony-full
solar system

bloomed into our palms,
            a crust of pollen,
            or comet dust,

or what you find under
the hood of a car
            a seven horse power car
            a herd of horses car

this horse a mare
we stared down in a field
until she loped to us,
                sweating,
                her will misshapen
                and smooth,
                her will gilled,

scale-crazy, glisten-morning,

like a trout

III. THIS DARK BOX/WHAT ABOUT THE MOTHS?

coffin   cold   a tangle of nurses   a wrangled flock of insects
shaking out their little insecty wings   all fluttery   crisp   and ready

IV. THE ROADS I DROVE

Pink   punch   drunk,   on the back of some four wheeler with a boy
I have loved since fifth grade, he's cutting down trees   on the weekends
and finishing school on Tuesday and Wednesday nights.   He reaches
up my shirt with his driving hand.   The other is his waving hand,
the one that could still be on the wheel. We veer into the river.
We veer into the past.   We veer into the ravine of sword ferns
where our friend   lost her life, where another broke   her hymen.
I want to kiss them: his diesel mouth,   her throat   of thorns. For him
I would swing an axe   at this beautiful cedar.   For me
he would cut down   the sun.

V. A CITY OF PETALS

This cemetery is a neighborhood of rhododendrons. A rhody is a flower that looks like a tongue. A tongue tells a secret of hums and vibrations. A hummingbird hovers, proboscis inside one pushed-open bloom. This headstone, covered in pollen so we can't see who's buried here— sweep off the stamens with a long-handled broom.

VI. THIS OLD CAR

the one you drive
when you can't saddle the horse

the one you pull from the bushes,
hook to jumper cables

the one you fly to Jupiter
so you can orbit

those rings like a race track,
your hair out the window,

your eyes on Jupiter's moons—
Ganymede, Callisto, Io, Europa

like a quartet of stone sisters
in their soft glide

around this striated pond
of foreign, unhinged glow

VII. ITS RUSTED AXLE

like a clicked tongue
come   unmoored
a cracked   board

unpeel me like a sticker
   from this page
of my life

like an unfixed   wife

this boat floating skyward
this boat floating darker
into dark earth

this boat a garden
of   slick   birth

& something unsaid

& something not wedded

to anything worldly
except dust   its floating
torn form

O flip this car over

O see the fireweed growing
through the floor boards

O how it whitens with
   heady   delight
& needs   wind
O the seed—

VIII. BACK ROADS, WINDING, NO GRID

Mapping the creased
streets of my mother's brain,

I stumble to a swaddled
bundle, lashed to that horse.

While the horse chews
my offer of carrots, her warm

breath still wet on my palm,
I unwrap the cloth

to find a baby, half human,
half fish, like a winged

girl with a question-mark
body, soft as sky, smooth

as ocean after sharp rain,
its muted salts.

How does a mermaid
arrive on a mainland?

How does a mother
keep her alive?

*

Reaching through the neck,
I pull wet stuff that fills

the eyes with illness—

RACHEL CONTRENI FLYNN

THE ORIOLE OUTSIDE MY WINDOW REMINDS ME

I have new birds. A new house. A new black
river full of silt   stars   peach   fruit   rich earth.

This is where you roamed in your youth, running
nude with the boys from high school, the ones

kinder than the boys in books who kill each other
for pride. I have nothing to wash off my hands,

nothing to scrub from my skin, no sin, no November
wind to snuff the candle. Still, I can feel it: my childhood

like heavy wood carried without a wheelbarrow.
A fire I will have to start, the flint in my pocket,

a locket full of worms. My ransom unearned.
My mother in the shed swinging the ax. My father

with his thin bottles in the trees. My raw knees.
Am I forced to take back what I said of the sky last

night? Was it not darker than a river, full of the dirt
shaken from stars? Was it peach like the fruits

that have already passed us, browned in the earth?
I want these new birds. I want them with my dirty

heart. I want them landing in my eyes, my candles,
my wheelbarrow of worms. I can feel it. The fire

keeps burning. I'm learning to turn it low, it's almost
cold. You stand near it, while the river swirls

around you. I touch your chest. You seem so clean.
I understand, or think I understand:

I have nothing. How can someone have nothing
to wash off her hands?

A LOVE STORY

I. (*impressionist story*)

Avenue   of small   yellow   smears.
A couple,   kissing,   by the creek.
Lantern-light on a bridge,   at night,
the water lit   by their glow.   Fellows
lounging   on benches,   bowler hats
and finches   imagined in the sweep
of trees.

I will walk this pond of lilies
until my feet turn pink.   I will mouth
at the seal   of this couple until
I become that girl, holding   her parasol
over us both,   waiting for our train
and our ballet   and all the women
in white dresses   to come down
from the golden hills above the water.

II. *(cubist story)*

Your two faces; an askance cat.
Keep strumming this defunct guitar,
the music bending into our closed
lips so they hum uncomfortable
rhythms stiffly. I think there's a bird
on your head. Why so sad? Do
you want me to keep scraping
the hair off your neck? Do you like
the way I am breaking your torso
in two? Play the piano so the floor
quakes. Play my heart like an echo,
stomp so my shoes angle and squeak.
I want to cut a peach with you. I want
to share this square of blue. Let's fuck
up the room. You be the lion. I'll be
the groom.

STILL LIFE WITH MATERNAL INSTINCTS

If the uterus is an upside-down pear.

If the uterus is an upside-down pear
and the egg is this bead

from the bracelet I gave to my daughter
who broke the bead
and the bracelet is all the other eggs

back in the ovaries and this snake
my son drags
around by the tail is the fallopian
tube on the left and this shoelace

or this ribbon or this stretched hair tie
is the other tube and
this play tool bench with its loose nuts
and its four hammers is my brain
or these couch springs my ribs

or this train table can be put together
in several ways
to represent my heart, my son charging
his magnetic engine over the button

that makes it clang and the torn chair
cushion is my abdomen and if the uterus
is an upside-down pear. If the pear,

here, is the still life, and this is the still life,
and life here is still. If still. If still.

If the pair of us said will. Is will still real?

ODE TO ALL THE WOMEN WHO WALK INTO THE LAKE AND SOME OF THE WOMEN WHO TAKE THEIR CHILDREN WITH THEM

Because they cannot stop for death
or the long sweeping parabola of the horizon

they weight their pockets with agates,
those dull burdens of light and ink, and wade in—

yesterday, the six-year-old said she missed
being in the womb, where no one bothered her

and the three-year-old
made a portrait of his mother with only two colors

and the brush strokes looked
like birds' wings, and the brush strokes looked like

fins, so why not climb out of her velvet dress
I mean cotton blouse I mean flannel pajama pants and jump

like Mary Poppins into the dream
of a different landscape? What if she really does

want to hold a parasol or even kill
foxes? Is it so easy to hate the women who abandon their
offspring

for pleasure or solace or the long sweeping
parabola of the horizon, to which they return like arrows

to their bows, or like horses
to the first hour after birth, their skin still glistening

with the chance of death, before walking,
when their legs were just four long appendages stretching

and wondering and being licked
and prodded by their own mothers' hopeful tongues?

"WHATEVER GETS THE HAY DOWN TO THE PONIES"

Eat the gold down to a corrugated core. To its cob. In an Iowa field, your grandmother, washing her clothes. In an Iowa field, your grandfather's union truck driving over the corn. The morning is warm, the sheets are warm. A begonia erupts by your grandmother's back door. Her screened-in porch. Your brother, torching the horse. Your mother, the horse. Tear the horse to open the storm. Your warm sheets. Sheets of rain. Rain floods the corn fields. Float like a rose on your back. Sink deep in Iowa mud. Your skull wet and warm. Your bullet hole skull. Eat the corn of your corrugated porch. Eat the dream of your yellow dance. Dance the day into Iowa. Have you been here before? Dream three fallow fields, three ears of corn. Intone them a song. This is the cob of your dream. Is this where you'll go when you're gone? Is this the grave of seed and throng, the dark shore and water of the deeper pond?

STORY PROBLEMS

The square root of whiskey is water. The square root of you is your father. You follow him down the hallway where he turns left and left again into a wall. He slumps there, half drunk. He stands, half awake. He banks his shot off the rail into the side pocket. It's cutthroat you're playing, not the fish, but the billiards game with the hard balls, the cue stick slightly warped so it wobbles when you check it. The square root of a cue is warped by water. The square root of Jesus is water into beer. That's the way the story is told here, where the square root of beer is your father, himself the square root of God. He knocks another in so you're stranded over here by the corner with your balls nearly touching like Adam reaching. Here, the square root of morning is Adam punching God in the face. In this part of America, Adam punches God in the face. It's almost morning; the sun sneaks around the darkness and creases in the blanket your mother hung to keep out the light. Somewhere above you stars blink off and you know there's work to be done, a cord of wood to split and stack, your brother's back to bend. The square root of your mother is waiting for you in the dim of her room, naming ferns for the sister you hope will come out of the woods. The trees there are square, their roots square, their leaves. You've been playing all night while the rain falls and the river swells higher. You may not make it home on these roads. You may find home in flames. But the billiards game: the name of the third player evades you. It may be the devil. It may be the square root of a story, an equation, an imaginary number spiraling off the edge of the page. Home may be the square root of these roads. The roads are full of the dark squares of sky they've been named for. In the field full of water where nothing is named for itself, the days are only hours long. You reach for your mother, who holds out a fern. It's a maidenhair. You're that close. You're drunk on the possibility of going somewhere. The square root of the river breaches the square roots of its banks.

JAKE, THE ALLIGATOR MAN

I.

I was afraid   of Jake
the Alligator Man:
his hands, like mine—
claws,   his decayed jaw
and shrunken eye sockets.

II.

When my parents no longer
owned the billiards hall
by the mattress store,
I wandered in Marsh's
Free Museum.

In Marsh's Free Museum,
you can find:
a lamb
            with eight legs
                        and one head,
free shells, Mary
            Lou's skeleton, discovered
                        in Aberdeen,
the store's pet cat Morris,
            orange and dead
                        and having met
                        his taxidermied fate,
and Jake—
the Alligator Man.

I was not afraid   of Jake.
We had nothing

in common, besides
the vestigial tail
and our affinity
for swampy water,
affection for Morris,
and fathers, probably,
in whom
we felt constantly
                disappointed.

III.

I found Jake in his case
and I let him out.

Jake jumped
when I broke the glass.
Jake went gallumping
on his four legs—two alligator
legs, two human arms—

through the dunes of wild
strawberries, beach grass,
to the shore where locals
and tourists
drove their big-tire   trucks
so they wedged, stuck

in the sand
in rows, a fence of metal
and its rusted grills.

My father would come later
with his hook and wench.

Jake crawled beneath,
slithering under axles
now,   snake-like,
snakey Jake   to the sea.

IV.

And what of me?
I'd used the *Test*
Your Love Power
coin-op machine,
knew mine
was sublime.

I ran, too, into the waves.
I was/wasn't afraid.
I knew Jake was out there,
like a merman,   waiting.

*

Silvia, Silvia, Silvia,
I met you in the belly of a whale—

MARISSA NADLER

IN THOSE EARLY DAYS, THE WOMAN WHO WAS A MERMAID DREAMS OF LONELINESS

Sometimes I pretend there is no one
in the next bed, that the light
through these windows comes only
for me, that the clicks
and whirs I hear are merely
the wind or some small bird
winding the clock. Then my roommate
groans and turns in her white sheet
and they come with their kind tray of new
pillowcases and she tells them
how, when the lights are out,
mine shines like blue milk, how it shimmers
with my hairs, which only results
in more meds for her and though
some part of me knows it is wrong,
I keep quiet. I have said nothing
this whole time. At night I lie with my feet
on my pillow so I can imagine it is a wave
and the moon is a ship or a cave or the full
eye of the squid, its inky sail behind it
like a prisoner. Those nights the fog
comes and freezes on the glittering
shingles of the solarium roof and I drink
my cold water slowly, as if this one glass
could, and were enough to, both
enter the body and surround the body,
the flesh less percent water than the space
around it, and therefore buoyant. I had a body
once that I could trust. The kind of trust
that goes beyond the rain, the kind
of trust with fins. But every day,
in this place with more rock
than water, I am scrubbing my brain.

WHEN SHE SWAM AMONG HORSES

Once, when the horses were around us,
    their teeth like buoyant pearls

above the nacreous waves, their eyes,
    too, like folded-open shells

and all that breath—hot, the steam,
    as if the ocean were on fire—

once, we felt less animal, as if we
    were the ones to blame for all the struggle

in the world, this, the herding of beasts,
    on their way from one island

to another, larger island. If this is what it meant
    to feel human, I wanted nothing of it.

I could be a whale, or crustacean,
    even, something armored and mute,

dreaming only of oxygen. It was my mother
    who swam beneath one of them then,

who encircled it in her arms so her hair—
    blue like water but not blue like water,

more like light, like the streaks light creates
    in large bodies of water—her hair

wove in vein-shapes on the horse-hide,
    so it was all river and delta from beneath

where my sisters and I swam, safely,
          watching the legs thrash and then not

thrash, but become steady, not mathematical
          but rhythmic and plant-like, a slow

and certain sway, even though they were still
          moving forward, that horse was going to reach

its destination, only less like a horse
          and more, now, like a dark-hoofed yellow god.

WHEN THEY SCANNED HER BRAIN FOR LOVE

It was the animal that came up
dominant. The animal who tears
across the lawn at dusk and leaps

into the pond. The animal who climbs
trees on the property perimeter,
who sleeps in the leaves,

dreaming of anemones and sea stars.
Who walks barefoot toward the sea.
I can hear it wrestling with the sand,

that old game, swallowing and choking on
and spitting out glass. It smooths,
but doesn't feel tender toward stones.

The sea came up dominant in me—
not a field, or sky. No wonder.
These qualities lie just beneath

the scalp — self-esteem, veneration,
benevolence. When they scanned
my brain for love they found only

my longing to come and go
and repeat. My currents pulled
by a world beyond the one

they know. I would pull
out my hair
for that world.

GARDEN THERAPY: SHE GROWS ASPARAGUS

In the moon-beds of the sea, deep glinting
flippers, bit-like, slight spears. If I turn away
under these stars, will the red-tipped
buds still bloom when I turn back?

At night, I watch myself glide
instead of wasting away the dream hours.
I can't help but bring time, bring bounty instead of waste.
I line the beds in rocks and eggshells, compost
gowns for these green ladies. Our teacher says,
allow them to establish their charms. We're
supposed to wait to harvest. To eat them, you slice
each green knife. But I don't want to. I want

to cut the hair from these dark graves.
The other girls have risen in their sleep, too,
all of us sleepwalking, aware to different states.

At intervals we walk the campus gardens,
follow one another, watch swallows,
forget where we are. We knit fingerless
gloves, our above-ground nourishment,
wondering who among us believes herself
a root seeking dark soil, impatient
as the sharp nettle. Sometimes I brush my skin

against each plant to see how my skin
will react, the rash narcissistic as silk. We wait.
We mulch heavily, as instructed. In the raised
bed like a grave our tubers' roots turn white

as worms. We lie down around the bed like mothers
who wait all night for their children to wake.

IN ART THERAPY, THEY HAVE HER SKETCH LEGS

It is easy to love their names, especially
those that run below the knees: *peroneus*

longus, tibialis anterior, gastrocnemius, calcaneal
tendon. I whisper them to myself as I draw

everything close to the feet, rubbing my pencil
on the paper in waves to make shadow, show

contour. See how she raises up on her toes now,
the flesh contracts, the shape between the legs

suggests a vase, I want to fill it with flowers.
I want to hold each calf in my hand, study

my favorite muscle. I put it on the page, instead:
soleus, Latin for sole fish. Dogs don't

have them. In horses, they're unused.
Which means they are somewhat particular

to homo sapiens. *Soleus*. Without it, we couldn't
run or dance. I have never gotten used to

how vertical I have to be all day, how limited
the angles are of the land-bound beings.

So it's a comfort that we might all have a fish
in our calves. I'd like to swim and let the fish

of my legs swim. I'd like to find out how to kick,
what kind of fin flip I would need. Will I ever

acclimate to walking? Will I always, standing
nude in front of the mirror, tremble in fear

at my own flesh, how it goes on and on,
pink and unscaled, from my head to my feet?

JANUARY 9, 1493: COLUMBUS MISTAKES MANATEES FOR MERMAIDS

What is there to love
          about Christopher Columbus?
By now we know he was a liar

through and through: pretending
          to have fallen into a new world
through the rabbit-hole of the ocean,

to have found this place where thousands
          already spent their days living,
where mountains knew the feeling

of feet on their backs. Or so I have
          read. I know so little. But I can tell you
Columbus told the truth

about one thing. Those were no
          manatees he saw off the coast
of the Dominican Republic. The story

goes that my great great great
          grandmother and her sisters swam
to see the ships with pretty rumors

for names and came back ashamed.
          So I've been marked with the curse
of curiosity. It's genetic. Once

I traveled to see the aftermath
          of a tsunami. I couldn't keep up
with the waves themselves. Water

is the only thing that can travel faster
            than a mermaid. The beach where
those large swaths of sea crashed

down was still awash in foam.
            There were dead babies, floating,
and I couldn't save them. No one

seemed to notice my fish
            tail, my glowing hair. They were
already in another world.

*

Sometimes I imagine the sea as a cauldron
I am making spells in

—

There is nothing more
pleasurable to me
than my ardent unavailability

AMY KEY

BOWL OF CLOCKS AND STONES

Friend E says you can have sex with the wind
from a phone booth on a cliff, the ocean below

rattling the receiver, the waves repeating. Maintains
you can say anything you want in a poem.

It's true I've been writing all these breathy epistolaries, for lack
of a better phrase. Again it's October, the month I repeat

like a wind in an open mouth. October, when my feet
always go grass-wet. I repeat the eleven-year refrain, pretending

at a season, when really the ode crashes out for your voice,
for whom half my words take shapes, for whom I unwind

from dreams, walk out into these still deer-studded trees, scatter apple
peels, pluck a stem of jeweled grapes. I read somewhere bare feet

on a woman make a man want to lie her down, so I keep
my shoes on when you're in town. Friend K once confessed

how disappointing were her husband's attempts, like all
men's, too warm, too hot, too there. She has to perform

all the magic. I think about being a man, how you must all forget
what it means to be deciduous. Today I peeled a hundred blue plums

remembering how good they tasted before my breasts
came in, when a field was just a golden receptacle of wind. My children

bring me a yellow bowl of water, full of stones and clocks,
the bridle from a toy horse. There's an elusive spell there,

like the wind entering all our bodies, filling our adult bones
with the weight of nothingness. What's that, Friend E?

Hold on, October. Hold on, wind. I'm listening. But she says go back
to you, my essential ghost, you're blowing away. Let it take off all

your leaves. Let me climb into your cold branches. Don't move.
I remember exactly where the holds are, I remember them in my bird

hollows, I have a place I like to perch, wait for the breeze.

SPELL FOR RE-MAKING THE PERSONAL ENVIRONMENTAL IMAGINATION

If, like Thoreau, you have three chairs,
make of them a triangle from which you can wander
into the night like a kitten looking for milk.

Wander, chair-less, bowl-less, into night, the moon always
ahead of you like a vowelly song.

You like being vowelly, your name a long vowel sound
held in by a moon. Hold your blood in
with the moon. Let your blood out
with the moon.

The thing is, when you're moony,
you want to be alone. The thing is, when you're holding
forth with the moon, sometimes you want a friend.
Sometimes you read to the deer
and sometimes you read to the grapes
and sometimes you read to your children.

It takes a lot of thinking hard about how the strawberries
send out their runners beyond their rocky border
for you to go out and talk to people.

Daily, you go out
and you talk to people, dragging that third
chair wherever you go, that chair like a chain
around your moony name.

You want to be more like the deer
and the ferns and the swallows taking
your hair clippings from where you cast
them beyond the grapes. You want to be more
grape-like, how they curl along the fence intimately,
how they hold the tree like snakes.

Daily you grow less like a plant and more like a person.
Deer confuse you in their daily paths.
Your daily path confuses you.
Though you have the moon, sometimes
when it turns red as blood,
you go out and you ask it
why it is a spherical drop of fluid, as a fat droplet in milk,
why, when kitten spent all night pursuing it
in *Kitten's First Full Moon*,
did it keep going and going and going
so all she could do was follow,

down the sidewalk,
through the garden,
past the field,
and by the pond,

until she had to climb a tree
and jump in?

SPELL FOR EXTROVERSION

It takes a lot of thinking hard about how the strawberries   send

their runners   beyond this rocky border   for me to go out and
    talk to people.
Unlike Thoreau, I have only one chair,
and I prefer to sit on the grass anyway, watch the ants crawl.
I said crawl, but sometimes they scurry,
and sometimes they carry things that weigh much
much more than the ants themselves weigh.

People have made of this a metaphor,
but that is making it about people,
not ants. If you consider every metaphor
as being really about the vehicle, not the tenor,
you will spend a lot of time in images,
and animals, and plants, and objects,
which, really, is where you'll find your time
best spent. Spend time in children's books:
a kitten and her moon, her bowl of moon milk.
A toad, his button jacket, a bird, running
toward the notion of a mother. It's the notion
of the mother that everyone carries around
all day like an empty dark pocket.

I am the notion of a mother. Instead,
I want the notion of a bird to take this notion
of my hair I've cast out beyond the grapes.
Take my hair and make a nest.
When I was a girl, my friend's mother said
her hair is a rat's nest.

Now I have a daughter and I try not to worry
about her hair.

I want us to be more like the deer
and the ferns and the flick
of the fern when rain falls. I want to keep thinking
about the strawberry runners. My daughter
and I go out daily to find those who escape
and we tuck them back into their beds.

SPELL FOR THE FACE OF TERRY SAWCHUK (1966) & FOR MEDUSA NEBULA

O brightness turned low   like a laptop screen   in the daylight

I confess I barely understand the universe   or even just this nebula discovered eleven years before
Terry's face bore so many sutures & was photographed for posterity

& what Terry has to do with us

I think is obvious   I know you're afraid of me   so terrified I might wildly confess all the things

smash the face of a rhetorical situation like a hand in a glove smashes into a cheekbone

like a violent confession   or unbrushed hair
I so love a wild confession   as much as a cup of coffee   so necessary to finish all the tasks

my blue heart beat beating   & you said yours was fleshy & fast   & you know alliteration
drives me wild   as do hyacinths & kelp

& code switching   & the face of Terry Sawchuk   before goalie masks

can you imagine how the pucks just Frankensteined a cheek   probably legendary

how the ice rink was a galaxy of collapsing stars

how my four-year-old wildly shoves handfuls of Cheerios into his open star hole

still intact & constellation, still throwing out light   probably legendary like the beast wandering the far north
seeking a nebula   sinking in his own despair

Images so piecemeal with borders

like this map we pretend means something

when we know the only borders are made of water & land

even those are no border, no *braided serpentine filaments of glowing gas*

& these suggest the hair of the goddess

& Sawchuk & Medusa & the monster all suffered from undiagnosed depression & how beautiful the fractured light & how this suggests

even the edge of you blurs with me   if we can just admit it   we'll be so much more
healthy   or we'll turn to stone completely   let's say everything

pulmonary embolism is a clot that moves from the lungs to the legs — a short lived phenomenon — like
electric colored light

I want to look through a telescope with you — or a microscope at you — dissect or discover or something
“masculine” — or

I just want to desire you less   finally banish the longing   I like the idea of a social experiment   &
of you remaining a fiction

wildly confessing   into the face of the goalie

who cannot stop everything with his beautiful pre-nebulous face

which at one point was something his mother invented   inside her ovary

ELLENSBURG IS THE WINDIEST MONTH: APRIL EDITION (SPELL FOR AURALOGY)

crab grass is another name for finger grass/ is another name for the spot of earth not scorched but colonized/ by grass/ every spring it has to re-seed & start over/ in those places it left barren/ which is another way of saying America/ & I'm so over you I'm flying/ I take a plane to another part of the country/ I take a boat to another part of the country/ look how lucky we are this place is fucking huge/ we're so fucking lucky/ our President drops a bomb & we call it a mother/ I think of calling you to say I told you so/ but I'm miles over your head now/ & I'm drinking from this reusable cup/ so responsible, I feel so responsible like a tortoise who waited/ I'm patiently waiting for things to reheat/& someone says something someone is thinking/ I'm so happy to witness the jinx/ & today the wind mills are moving at 75 mph, making so much electricity/ did you know the little bunnies are thriving in their undercarriage/ I am so glad to not be thinking of fucking like bunnies/ hawks really struggle not to be chopped to shreds by those giant blades/ the bunnies can't hear anything though / in their metal-turbine havens/ no carnivore is bothering them/ except us in the future/ in their metal-turbine hell bushes/ in our sage brush bungalows/ no claws swooping in/ & they're quietly fucking like bunnies/ making more bunnies/ & a lap top is a creature/ like an inbred dog/ small, warm bowels on your knees/ waiting for you to finish your coffee

SPELL FOR THEIR BELLY BUTTONS/ WITH A DICTIONARY CLOGGING ITS WINDPIPE

it's a pretty simple story/ anyone could tell it/ we were trying to come up with my Latin name & E said it's obviously umbilicus something/ I was like maybe it's barnus umbilicus or riparius barnicus/ both invoke barnacles & their feathery protrusions/ invoke cords carrying blood/ invoke rivers & barns/

& driving past a Tyrannosaurus Rex on the side of a pole building we settled on riparius umbilicus/

when I was a gastropod things were pretty hard for me/ & I had a distinct opening

sounds better than umbilicus/ maybe it does/ but then again a river is always connected to its source/ ha ha geology jokes/ & all you need is *Moh scale*

In English, mostly confined to medical writing

when I was a squirrel I was beautiful & I never even thought of the buttons

this week a giraffe had a giraffe in a box/ I know very little about it/ I admire the spots but I can't click on the story/ it repulses me in its affectations/ I know the bark is falling off the trees in the burn zone/ & I don't know if it's from being so hot or from beetles/ I fear the trees are going nuclear/ like a president or dictator/ what's the difference between the insects laying eggs in your curtains/ & the mammal working so hard to promote Toys "R" Us/

& all of the following are true:

> 1. *historical example: The shell is thick, imperforate (no umbilicus), and usually has flat, spiral ribs*
> 2. *origin: Botany, zoology. a navel-like formation, as the hilum of a seed*
> 3. *historical example: In this case the shell is said to be umbilicated, and the opening referred to is the umbilicus*

& standing around after the reading my students say *you're like the mom*/ I cringe & the male professor laughs/ doubling across his own umbilicus/ forgetting his mother/ I'm always forgetting my mother/ we're all guilty of erasing our mothers/ their ribs & their openings

in biology umbilicus is also the *hollow or navel-like structure, such as the cavity at the base of a gastropod shell* / a shell is also a fine place to raise a child/ if you're a child/ or a hermit crab/ or a person afraid of the underground/ & the stratosphere

This experience is called a parade/ & I am plunging the future for its clogged pipe/ & this is called a routine/ & umbilicus has a root word named [   ]/ & when you kiss their faces when they are sleeping they still move their lips in a nursing motion/ it's the same shape as a tree knot/ & this is what I call photosynthesis/

& when I was a tree I aspirated daily/ it wasn't even dangerous/ & this is a supple climbing branch/ aka a magic portal/ this is how I got on the float/ I pretty much aced the application/ for the first time in a long time I wasn't even overqualified/ if anything I was lacking/ save me a spot at our regular table

& when I was the wind I was terrible/ always ripping out root systems/ now that I'm a mother/ I'm always plugging them back in/ transplanting is another word for it/ umbilicus has a root word & it is *umbilicus*/ in the Latin its origin is *navel, middle, center/ compare Latin umbō shield boss*/ if you unfold the world map the western way the Latin is right in the middle/ like an American gazing at herself/ guilty as a writing "student"/ on the other side of the cord/ guilty of everything for which I was accused/ get me a letter for my chest/ make it a giant U/ better yet pin it on my belly/ now this is what I'd call a party/ we'll need to begin taking turns/ the mansion has so many rooms left to be cleaned/ scrub them down with a bucket of salt & old stars/ & you know ratty underpants & undarnable socks/ make great furniture polishers/ get yr Swiffer it's gonna be a long party/ we have so many floors to shine with the afterbirth

SPELL FOR HIGHLY CAPABLE CHILDREN/ & NEWBORN GIRAFFES / & GAFFES

my highly capable children are barely capable of swiping a condensed bunch of plastic bristles across their glossy calcium/ aka tooth brushing/ aka rinse and spit/ into the highly glossy ceramic bowl

I just can't read any more about this poetic giraffe/ I'm more interested in the forsythia outside my window/ without hovering supervision

my children are highly capable of using an iPad/ their grandma looks at them with wonder/ says they'll need to learn to use it for school/ so let's start when they are twenty four months/ eventually you'll need to indoctrinate them with cheeseburgers & synthetic fabrics/ she says/ she says it's so convenient

here I go again being mean/ breaking the first rule of nonfiction/ like someone mocking a first generation college student/ my friend E says what's with all the proud parent sweatshirts/ before she realizes their parents didn't attend university/ she'll kill me if she sees what I've written here about her/

& I need to write out a full apology to everyone/ but I'm more interested in the rain barrel as an illegal enterprise it's amazing how many things we've outlawed for the environmentally conscious/ how we create elitisms of midwifery/ how we say foraging when we mean finding food/ how we say tiny home when we mean house

do I sound yet like an adventure capitalist/ do I sound yet like a libertarian/ letting down her hair/ are libertarian women allowed to let down their hair?/ there I go again/ getting myself in trouble for microaggressions/ once I was a girlfriend/ of a person who said *now you're crossing a line*/ he was my friend but also we were kissing/ over a long distance line/ calling myself his girlfriend is part of the bigger problem/ so is saying *long distance*/ we never had a clear break up/ it was more silty like a river that runs backward/ flooding & regressive politics are both things that happen in patterns/ glacial melting is a consequence of highly capable children

I prefer not to label myself but if I must let's go with independent/ let's go with riparius umbilicus/ it's a term for a poet who was born in an ocean/ it's a term for a poet born in a gas station

without any drugs except daily use of marijuana, negative ions, & gasoline/ how they paid the midwives

O blue planet I wanted to tell you/ I was born huffing/ my own kind of bowl

*

Think of all the fun I've had
It's hard to feel less than glad
Then again I'm completely mad

We're all mad here

EMMA WALLACE

OUT-TAKE AS A DREAM OF CHILDREN

You say marrow   I say dress
marrow   dress
marrow   dress

You say cephalopod
I say triceratops

You change colors faster than a chameleon
while scientists debate over my horns and frills
and I wear my face to prom
my prom of the three horned face

I promenade at prom while you scrape bones
along the floor. This floor is made of bones.
This floor is home. This floor is home.

You jump out the window into the ocean
where every seventh wave crashes whiter to the right
along the ropes we've set out to measure them

and you can hold the rope with one of your eight arms
and I can face the window with my three horns

and they can make my face a tiara
and your arms a dress

that clings to bone.

You say marrow   I say dress
marrow dress
marrow dress

You say squid   I say marry
squid   marry
squid   marry

Nautilus cuttlefishoctopus

I want to die   I want to die in your eight arms
and be carried into the bone floor
your bone floor
your floor of bones
your arms of lace
facing me in my tight white dress

OUT-TAKE AS A CURL OF DUSK

Hours of sun, thorns in the dark gold sword of day. A field, shark-jawed and raw with skin and hair and insects. After this flesh has gone cold, scattered in dirt, across hills, forests, clacked away from us, or what we've become, after our children even sag with age and longing, will we miss the black fabric of sex, like a dull beer still desired, or will we be so beyond it, beyond like the enchanted castle lies beyond the briars, sleeping for a hundred years, having forgotten the dream of the sole kiss that could wake it?

OUT-TAKE AS A SONNET OF WAR

The severed deer leg said *red*,
as if red were something to be said.

My head fell off and rolled over the mossy
embankment. I followed, my neck austere

and cold and salmonberry-covered, running
with a colored orange and the yellow sun

coming up over the edge of the canyon
though we could not see the canyon

and even if we could wouldn't we have leapt
into it? I carried the deer's body, I kept

checking to see if its heart still beat.
Meanwhile behind me the bombs retreated

into the fog and I could hear my mother
hum: *Don't you have a brother*

out there, too? Do you want to know
how we're all doing? So I'm going

to check with those in charge, I'm asking
the questions, even if I get answers.

Meanwhile my trachea began to close,
shiver and shiver and open. Meanwhile

I tore off the deer's head, attached it
to the stump of my own neck.

OUT-TAKE AS A DREAM OF RHODODENDRONS

Oh wet vertebrae,   rescue sweet,
    dirt flecked and pink.

Your pink flecked throats. Your roads
    of sweet Oh.

Your thick youthful   blooms in June,
    slick, dewy as lilacs.

Because it was always   raining & you were always
    wet, pink or fuchsia,

the color, not the flower,   on your waxy green
    leaves. You in a row

on the high school lawn.   And fawns, foraging
    mouths. Your underbrush.

Picked, you brown   quickly; no one ever
    tried to flatter a girl

with a bouquet   of your blooms. But
    make out by a rhody

and they say you'll   lose your virginity.
    It's easy. Do they say that?

Do I remember? Rhododendron, state
    flower, your white

neck, kissed and kissed   again, sweet vertebrae
    of your stem, your branches

grown wild and large   in these temperate
            rain forests, let me sit

a while in your shade,   the damp dirt beneath
            you, the rescue

of your sticky blossoms   strewn here like girls'
            panties, the kind

who were pregnant   before they graduated,
            the kind who bloomed

and made us jealous   with their blooming,
            who knew to brush

the stamens from their jeans   before rejoining us
            for lunch, no trace

of rhodies on them,   while I tried once
            skipping class

with a friend, was found before lunch was over,
            rhododendron stamens

and their thin brown   blooms stuck like lies
            to my canvas shoes.

OUT-TAKE AS A NARROW DRESS

Therianthropy: the man becomes
  the beast. A woman's flesh
unfolds to reveal a skirt of thorns.

Her skirt unfolds to reveal fire.
  Her fire rips at the door.
Her door opens, a beast

leaps onto the page. The sheets
  peel back like skin, we're in
the bed, they and I, a skirt

of horns. What is borne
  in the brain becomes
bone. What strains at its ropes

is my brain. Therianthropy,
  they say, is my desire
to be animal. *That* isn't it.

Have you ever looked so hard
  through leaves they all become
eyes? Have your eyes

grown leaves in their looking?
  I lay my leaves flat.
I layer them, one on another.

What does this look like
  to you? Can you smell fear
on my breath? The beast

turns female. She pulls
            her heavy body across
the beach. She finds herself

in a city of thorns, torn
            open, her bones open,
her sparrow homes,

her song of leaves.
            Her fired skirt.
Her small, smoldering dress.

OUT-TAKE/ STORYBOARD

What I mean to say is
being a mother made me feel
like a myth. What I mean is
I'm a fish. What I mean
to say is *don't open me.*
As in, I've always been folded
like a letter into its envelope,
smudged pencil, a scent of old wood,
language in its dark furnace,
something to say to someone,
flint-ready, char cloth,
waiting to burn.

ACKNOWLEDGMENTS

I am grateful to the editors of the following publications, where these poems first appear:

All We Can Hold: An Anthology of Poems on Motherhood: "Ode to All the Women Who Walk into the Lake and Some of the Women Who Take Their Children with Them"
Blackbird: "Spell for their Belly Buttons/ With a Dictionary Clogging its Windpipe"'
The Compass: "In Art Therapy, they Have Her Sketch Legs"
Tahoma Literary Review: "The Oriole outside My Window Reminds Me"
Floating Bridge Review: "In Those Early Days, the Woman Who Was a Mermaid Dreams of Loneliness"
Juked: "Documentary," "Out-takes from the Making: My Used Little Ovaries, The Horse We Opened Together, This Dark Box/What About the Moths?, The Roads I Drove, A City of Petals, This Old Car, Its Rusted Axle, Back Roads, Winding, No Grid," "Storyboard," "Still Life with Maternal Instincts," "Out-take As a Dream of Children"
Lilac City Fairy Tales: Vol. 1: "When They Scanned Her Brain for Love," "January 9, 1493: Columbus Mistakes Manatees for Mermaids"
Lilac City Fairy Tales: Vol. 2, Marry a Monster: "Out-take as A Narrow Dress," "Out-take As A Dream of Children"
Pleiades: "Story Problems"
River Mouth Review: "Spell for Extroversion"
Spokane-Coeur d' Alene Living Magazine: "Field Girl Come Home"
Tusculum Review: "Out-take As a Curl of Dusk"

This book is for my children, Zoey and Canyon. May you document all the dirt and all the wonder.

Much gratitude to Eduardo Corral, for believing in this manuscript and selecting it for the New American Poetry Prize, to David Bowen, for sending it to Eduardo, and to everyone who ferried it on its way, especially Angelo for his perfectly strange collage work and design, and Carol Guess, Laura Read, and Diane Seuss for writing blurb copy that sees the book with incisive and tender care.

I am also grateful for the Sustainable Arts Foundation, for believing parenthood and writing can co-exist, to the Centrum Foundation, for the gifts of time and spell-ingredients, to the H.J. Andrews Experimental Forest, for creating places for artists and scientists to cross pollinate, and to the Inland Northwest Jellyfish Collective, Kat, Ellen, and Laura: may we find ourselves in one another's many arms for years to come.

To Sharma Shields, fairy mud-mother: thank you for encouraging mermaid poems and other magic. For curating the great cauldron.

My sincere debt to the ancestry of poets who precede us all and those today who work to make more seats at the table and paths in the field. Most especially, thank you to those whose backing of my projects and/or time with poems helped hold space for this book: Taneum Bambrick, Dawn Pichon Barron, CMarie Fuhrman, Knox Gardner, Christine Holbert, Ellie & Jonah Kozlowski, Kate Lebo, Matt Martinson, Rachel Mehl, Kathryn Nuernberger, Laura Read, Liz Rognes, Michael Schmeltzer, Kathryn Smith, Torrey Smith, Karaline Stamper, Ellen Welcker. You wondrous room of alchemists; I love you all.

NOTES

"Field Girl Come Home," the line "this is the moment you learn what you'll love," is modified from Dorianne Laux's lines "this is the moment/ when I learned what I would love," in her poem "Homecoming."

"As Documentary" owes its origin to Robin Ekiss's poem "The Question of My Mother."

The first line of "Ode to All the Women..." is a paraphrase of Emily Dickinson's line "Because I cannot stop for death."

"In Those Early Days, The Woman Who Was a Mermaid Dreams of Loneliness" takes and adapts four lines from Ashley Capps' book *Mistaking the Sea for Green Fields*.

"When They Scanned Her Brain for Love" was inspired by the image of the brain appearing in the Encyclopedia Britannica, which explains Viennese doctor Franz Joseph Gall's concept of phrenology, the pseudo-science of the conformation of the skull.

"Ellensburg is the windiest month..." contains a line from my collaboration, *Alchemy for Cells & Other Beasts*: *"I'm so over you I'm flying"*

"Spell for their Belly Buttons" & "Spell for Highly Capable Children" both reference the giraffe, who, in April 2017, gave birth on live camera: "April's celebrity and the public fascination with her unborn calf blossomed when the zoo began providing a live YouTube stream in February...Hundreds of thousands of viewers have watched the 15-year-old April since then, and more than a million people witnessed the birth on the livestream" (Reuters).

Maya Jewell Zeller is the author of the interdisciplinary collaboration *Alchemy For Cells & Other Beasts*, the chapbook *Yesterday, the Bees*, and the poetry collection *Rust Fish*. With Sharma Shields, Maya co-edited the anthology *Evergreen: Grim Tales & Verses from the Gloomy Northwest*, and with Kathryn Nuernberger, co-wrote *Advanced Poetry: A Writer's Guide and Anthology* (forthcoming from Bloomsbury UK, January 2024). Maya teaches English for Central Washington University, as well as the low-residency MFA of Western Colorado University.

www.ingramcontent.com/pod-product-compliance
Lightning Source LLC
LaVergne TN
LVHW052343100826
845147LV00021B/1163

* 9 7 8 1 9 4 1 5 6 1 3 1 7 *